THE MAD RACE

GOUSIA SIDDICK

This book is written in gratitude to all those wonderful people who have been with me in my worst; Who probably, I will never be able to thank enough. I hope that the words I write here reflect the gratitude, the love and the respect I hold in my heart.

Special thanks to **Dr G. MadhuShankar,Dr Jayakumar** and all the other members of **Sri Ramakrishna Hospital, Coimbatore**; who have travelled with me in this journey of highs and lows and helped me understand that no disease can kill a man's indomitable spirit.

This is for you

May every word you read here bring you

strength and love from within.

You know what you endure and I

assure you that come what may

I am with you in this journey called

LIFE

Contents

Preface

Life is a perfect swirl; it moves in full swing with one center. This center is you. Is me. Is every individual who lives. Time passes and we know not where we are headed. There is joy and bliss, anguish and pain. This little book is dedicated to all those who are battling some pain, either physical, mental or emotional. Some pain that is quietly engulfing us within itself We know not and days pass by.

I was lost in a big battle of emotions last year. I was physically deteriorating; my body was failing hard. I had support, a lot of emotional support from those around me. I had to take decisions that would take me far, that would give me a second chance but I was scared. These decisions I would take will not be just mine but also impact those who I deeply loved.

My doctors assured me that all would be well. There was still that something I lacked. I pondered and found that I still needed that one voice, that voice which would give me strength. The voice I could rely wholly on. It had to be familiar. It had to be loud, so much that that it would echo from within me and resonate through me. This voice had to be mine.

This book is an attempt to help you and guide you as you face your battles. Those battles that do not allow you sleep and pinch cells within you. The pain that you hide behind tears keeping in mind those around you. This book is to help you find your voice, your journey within.

CHAPTER ONE

LOVE

"You yourself, as much as anybody in the entire universe, deserve your love and affection." - Buddha

I sat there looking at all those sullen faces who had pain in them. Their bodies looked fine. No scars, no tears but a grief so strong that their eyes carried it in them. A loved one was in there, in an ICU and here they sat just outside it not expecting anything other than a loved one well -being. In the hands of some was a rosary, a few hands had been crossed and heads hung low as if asking the universe where did they go wrong. The tears not outside their eyes but within them drenching their souls.

I sat with them thinking was my family going through the same. Did I make a mistake somewhere that I made them sit here for me? I could not quantify whose pain was more. Mine was insignificant in front of that I saw in her eyes. Maybe that is why she bore. I probably understood what saints said of poets sang of when they said "the eyes speak."

In a dilemma of self and taking a stride on my new understanding of love I began to think – Why does the heart longs for love. When the skies are grey, why do we look at days that have passed. Why do we reminiscence those innocent childish infatuations. That adolescence where love was a mirage of perfection and joy. Where are those days where we studied and wanted to support our dreams and pursue our brave career choices. Where is that perfect partner, we hoped to spend the rest of our lives with. Thinking of all those days and trying to quantify this seamless extent of feeling into days, hours and minutes not knowing for how long would we have to hold this to was indeed a strange feeling.

Some experiences are unexpected, they shape us into a new pitcher that was not planned to carry what it generally does but to alter its shape into whatever is poured into us. Getting smitten by the present, looking all around and seeing what I have in hand made realize that I had love, from people who spoke to me, from those around me but there was something still holding me back.

I got an understanding that I have to make myself familiar with these new settings. Now this wasn't a place I would hop in once in a while to see if I was working alright but a place that was there to ensure that I really am. It was difficult. It was challenging. I writhed in pain as I heard names of diseases, symptoms I had missed out and injections and needles. I was shifting in and out of thought and the mortal being I was.

With analgesics trying to make comfortable, I was again lost in deep thought. I was alone, with people around me. I was thinking of loved ones and love all around me but seldom did I think if I really loved myself. Self-love is something that has hardly crossed my mind. Love is not that happens with others. It is a conscious thought that I need to focus on and had in all these years failed to think about. It is an important and intimate. How I love myself and value myself is how I will treat others because I understand that they value themselves a lot too. It is a relationship I share with myself setting me as a high priority and telling myself that I am the charioteer of my life.

Self-love is not selfish

Thoughts that we share with ourselves have a extensive impact on the way our body reacts. A person in an emergency room surrounded by strange people trying to bring him under control cannot if he doesn't cooperate. He has a will to live and works with people to help him get back on track. These people in white coats slog in for years trying to save you and imagine you are physically well and you just do not love yourself. It is like fuel in the vehicle and not starting it.

You may wonder. Ask yourself. When is the last time I pampered myself? Working for kids all day long, When did I actually play with them? When did I take a long walk? When did I do something I love? Trust me, its therapeutic. My days in the wards of a hospital that who I now feel I am a part of brough to light so many things that I otherwise never thought of.

I heard a speaker say, "When you pass your old school, you tell your friends this is where I studied? Do you ever tell your friends proudly, happily this is where I was when I had this accident? You do not want to think about it because it bring bad and painful memories." Maybe yes, but when I hear the name of my hospital, I feel grateful. When I hear my doctors' names, I feel proud. I feel they are my people. Will I not be proud if my family member succeeds? This is not because they cured me or made me well but because of how they treated me. I was through multiple departments and I was treated as an individual, who had opinions and thoughts and ideas and I wasn't Pavlov's subject of study.

Something as simple as "I am happy" or "Yes, I am strong" rewires our thought process. You might wonder, how is this going to help me when I am suffering from a chronic disease or when I am in pain. I have been through it. Telling yourself "I think I can handle this" has had a great impact on the way I looked at things and the confidence it gave me is astounding.

Some simple affirmations on Self-love may be:

I am loved

I am whole

I am happy

I am doing the best I can

I can handle this

I love my body

I am doing a great job

My body is doing so well

This one aspect of embracing trials and loving yourself will strengthen your core and tell you that you have magic within. You have the ability to shift your locus to your center. You drive the energy around you. You are capable of infinite things. You are a wonder. Your life revolves around you. Your thoughts carve your path.

You are capable of making your loved ones smile. You have the capacity of enduring what is happening to you. The pain chose you because you have the strength to handle it. It makes you stronger. With love, you can direct your life.

This love is no longer dependent on external factors but is intrinsic. This love can move mountains. Remember, you are an ocean of love. The heart stops searching for love outside and attracts what is meant to be. This love is seamless. This is you. If anything beyond what you predict happens, it is the love of the universe for you.

CHAPTER TWO

THE ART OF LETTING GO

"Life teaches you the art of letting go in every event. When you have learnt to let go, you will be joyful, and as you start being joyful, more will be given to you" - Sri Sri Ravi Shankar

We are blessed with the power to think and to create. All that we do is a product of thought. Our thoughts have weighed us down so much that we have got used to carrying this burden of why, what, when, where and how all the time.

I was in a general ward where the person in the cot next to mine was reading a book. One might think what's strange about it. It was a local magazine. He would read, put the magazine down, close his eyes and either ponder or smile to himself. I was now curious, I asked what he was doing and he said there so much in this book. I can't think enough. He smiled, turned and continued.

This made me think, my, this man thinks so much even on little things. Science might argue that if not for that, we might not progress. I agree that it is important for one to be reasonably practical and be necessarily aware of what we are doing and the effects it has on us. Also, it is important for us to not be burdened so much that we forget to live in the moment.

If every individual keeps lingering only on the 'ifs and buts', will we actually move ahead? It is important to live in the present. Carpe Diem. One important lesson I learnt is that during hardship is that there are certain things that no one can share or take away from us. Live that second. It creates an irrevocable change and a chain of events that follow.

Everything that gives us pain is a pattern created not by the actual event itself but by the thoughts of it reoccurring in our minds. Holding onto things, thoughts, memories, basically anything that gives us pain doesn't yield anything. We need to let go. Let go of everything that weighs us down. In times of distress, a 'why me' usually steps in. Acceptance, knowing you are there for a reason and counting on to the endurance you have is even more powerful.

We need to stop expecting and live life as it is presented to us, we will see that we are indeed among the blessed. I do not say that we will not feel low. Being sad is natural. Being grateful is a choice. Being able to smile in pain is a choice that changes perspective and makes it easier for those around us; a choice that strengthens us.

My hardship taught me to count all the blessings I was bestowed with and within a year the way I looked at life changed. I subconsciously started embracing the little joys of life. I looked the brighter side of every aspect. I fall in love with the sunshine, the days, the nights, the different experiences, and people who made a difference, little magical things that were there but I had hardly taken time to notice. I became self-aware. I did not care if my cup was half empty or half full, I felt lucky to have the cup.

Minimalism became even close.

The journey was not easy and neither is. I am ridiculed for being crazy and embracing things that are not acceptable in my society. But, I alone know what life meant and what mattered when I was at the brink. Things where not humungous from a medical perspective but we live it, and we feel the pain around us as much as in us.

I let go of all those things that where not in my control and I realized the positive impact it had on me. I let go of stress, of habits that yielded no good, of irritation, of frustration and most importantly of fear. I started embracing the fact that whatever happens will be for my highest good.

Letting go of everything and embracing things as they were presented to me helped me understand that anticipation, expectation and fear is in no way going to help me anyway. My thoughts and the way I looked at life and embraced life definitely caused a radical shift in all I incurred.

Let go, embrace accept and be present in the now. Relish every moment and fear not for what happens is always for the highest good. Loose not this very second. Do your best now, the rest will follow.

CHAPTER THREE

FEAR

"Nothing in life is to be feared. It is only to be understood"
- Marie Curie

He took a sharp turn, he had to be on time. It was the first time, he had looked into her eyes. This was different. It gave him a sense of power. The power to live up to her expectations. To safeguard her. To love her. To be there for her. He remembered the moment where the vermillion from his fingers dropped on her straight parted hair. He loved her. He wanted to be there that evening with her. He had booked a table at her favorite restaurant.

It was the same route that he took every evening after work. He would wind up work by 5 PM. Walk down to the basement and drive out taking a sharp left turn from the building. The lavender of the building was his second home. As the clock at home struck 5, she knew, he had started and in 45 minutes he would be there.

Today was different, she smiled knowing that he would do something crazy just for her. He wasn't there at the usual time. She waited. It was 6:10 PM. Worried now, she sat, a little confused. Her face went blank when she received a call from the same lavender office he loved so much. There stood fear in front of her pale face.

We all love life. When faced with some kind of a danger, threat or loss, there is an unpleasant reaction called fear. Fear is natural. Either physical or psychological, we have faced fear sometime or the other. All problems we face are somewhere rooted in fear. We have a fear of failure, fear of abandonment, fear of loss, and yes fear of death. So, basically we have a fear of everything that doesn't happen the way we want it to.

The best part is no matter how strong we are, fear always comes in uninvited. We are left with either subduing it or facing it. One always feels better than the other. When there was fear right in front of me looking straight in me. The empath that I am, looked at fear and invited it for a coffee date. I think the best way to know someone is to talk over a cup of coffee.

I wanted to understand what is the problem? What am I actually being afraid of? The more I understood, there was lesser to be afraid of. I started putting together pieces of myself while pondering that no one would know me better than me. I let my physicians do their work. They were best at what they did. I just wanted to do my part. No big surprise there, I trusted them, their process, and co-operated with them. My fear told me, you either give up or stand firm. This gradual desensitization made me what I am today almost a year later.

I have been labelled as a patient with Systemic Lupus Erythematosus (SLE). It did teach me to patient though. Years of understanding lupus from a patient perspective helped me understand what I was going through and helped my doctor understand me better. I shared a lot of stuff with my doctor and I was wrong. My doctor was way more patient than I was. Lupus helped me understand what auto immune meant, what I needed to avoid and what would basically keep me going.

All was good until it progressed to End stage renal disease (ESRD). Like I said, my doctor was an epitome of patience. He ensured I understood what was happening and what would be the right way to proceed. Decisions about my body, my life were taken and I wanted to be present in it. That is exactly what happened and it felt great as I was not being pushed into something. I was being understood.

This, not only did help me understand the plan of action but also slowly helped me eradicate the sub conscious and hidden fear that was built up in me. I knew why a particular test was being done, what the results would mean and how I had to cooperate to get maximum results.

This is not as easy as it sounds, credits to my doctors who tolerated my tantrums that were a product of pain and hallucinations. I was made to understand what was done, and this contributed to a great extent towards my wellbeing.

It is always advisable only to know about it and to follow one's doctor's advice under all circumstances and take no personal decisions.

My conversation with fear is listed here. I know it was a bit personal but I am sure this would benefit you too.

1. What am I afraid of?
2. Why do you haunt me?
3. Will you leave? If yes, How?
4. What weighs more – benefits or effects?
5. Do you do me good or not?
6. Is this normal?
7. Is it ok to be scared?

This analysis helped me understand that there are a lot of unpleasant things that I may not like and I am likely to be afraid of it. But, if someone is taking a genuine effort in order to help me out, then the least I can probably do is to work with them so I be at peace and encounter less suffering than I currently do.

CHAPTER FOUR

THE CALM

Each one has to find his peace from within. And peace to be real should be unaffected from outside circumstances"
– Mahatma Gandhi

When we talk of peace, we would normally picturize sages wearing saffron sitting on mountain peaks. Is peace that difficult a pursuit? It is, when there is chaos all around you right. When there are frequent emotional outbursts and you suddenly are the center of attention. Or, is it atill untapped within you?

In situations concerning one's health, one may feel himself in extreme chaos. This confusion disrupts inner peace. A feeling of not wanting to be present, a feeling of shame and guilt so overwhelming that peace is found nowhere near.

It is important to be aware of these angry depressed feelings, but it is equally important to acknowledge and bypass them. There is no point in worrying about circumstances or people, the best would be to just be mindful of oneself. Deep within all that chaos is a locus, and in it is peace.

I understand this is not easy as said. Acceptance is the key to maintain a standstill in times that seem to tear apart the underlying strength. Looking from the outside it sounds too exaggerating but for one who lives every second of his life with thoughts that bring him to his lowest these things do matter. If you can rewire yourself, condition your mind to gather all that courage and smile, it is totally worth it.

Stability inside is like that tip of a top, no matter how much the top rotates it is all beautifully balanced. You suddenly gain a sense of awareness that this too shall pass. Everything seems so momentous. There is a feeling of disconnect. You are with everyone and yet long for the void. The absence of everything is desired. Here, you sense the calm.

CHAPTER FIVE

POWER

The past has no power over the present moment" Eckhart Tolle

When there is a desire to get something that we want, and the desire is deep; so deep that it transforms to into power. A power that can push you to reach the stars; to delve into the vastness of the skies. This power in concoction with the will is the real will power.

This secret cannot be found outside. It lies within the oceanic waves of serenity that encapsulates our soul. We live with it everyday. When we push our desire for strength of life, desire to overcome pain and difficulty, we give awaken it charging us to live, face trials, and achieve triumph.

Life is a beautiful game where not everything is played fair and square. Our minds are thirsty. We search for something that will quench our thirst. Money, power, pelf; something that will set us apart the ordinary. Once satiated, we move on and lo the thirst too. Newer things replace older hungers. This marathon continues for days, months and years, till the runner wears off.

Looking back, we lose track of all that we have always wanted. The need for survival entangles us and keeps us distracted throughout. We have been going on and on in circles. What about those million dreams that kept us awake? "Where has the power gone?"; just exactly where the desire has.

Sitting in the midst of people fighting their battles alome, trying hard to smile, is not the time to think about the fine sand slipping away from the crevices when we had full control. There is breath and we still have charge. We still can set things straight. All we need is that spark that decodes this power. When this want is strong enough, power comes from within.

What is braver than a smile when in pain. Feel the pain, rushing through every vein. Feel it travel deep in you. Tell yourself "I am stronger than this." Trust your physicians when they say you can manage this. All around you in that room, is pain and distress, it is only in his eyes we find trust and reassurance. I wish doctors knew the amount of hope and impact they imprint on every person they meet. They have this enormous energy in them to change mindsets. It is not just the medicine that works but the eyes that create a vision of wellness; the words that reflect positivity and the aura of a good heart that cares.

In a million people who exist in this world, why do you think only a handful paths cross. Some stay with us for days, as in a workshop or a camp. Few for years, classmates for instance. How many of our classmates are we in touch with? We probably spent our entire childhood with them. Today we hardly get to talk to them.

There are very few constantly in our minds. These are people who make a difference in our lives. They become friends who last a lifetime. Out of nowhere come these doctors who suddenly cross our paths. we listen to what they have to say. We follow their advice. They become, in a few visits, not even summing up to an entire day in the beginning become an integral part of our lives.

No wonder they are held in such regard. Let us trust them. Arjuna too chose Krishna, it is in tough times that we need guidance. When we do, we have a pillar to hold onto. We have someone who understands what we go through, diagnoses us with expertise. This trust is a form of power that kindles inside us constantly, day by day, week by week, during every dialysis telling us that we are well. There is no power stronger than that is inside you. This voice gives your power optimum strength.

Accept the present, believe in yourself. If there is a key to your troubles, it is within you. Call forth your strength. Trust people who work for your wellbeing. Surround yourself with positive energy. Give your body the energy it requires. Strengthen yourself from within. Shun not your soul. Trust the process. All that happens is for the highest good. When you are well, your heart will want to show its gratitude. When things because easy for you, your soul will thank endlessly.